Contents

Dear Carole,

And Ophelia, who answers to Fifi, but also to 'where's white mousy' and the sound of the food bowl. Well, she is the reason that I have not answered your email until now.

She is wonderful – all that you could hope for in a cat. Affectionate, clean, undemanding, playful, and entertaining.

But she bites. In her seventeen days here, she has attempted this four times, twice stopping herself, once drawing blood from both the top and bottom of my hand where she had sunk her teeth. The fourth time, two days ago, she by mistake bit the remote control that I was holding. It's a pity it wasn't 'live'. That might have been a strong lesson. There seems to be no reason why she should do this, but it is a big defect and probably the reason why she is looking for a new home. The RSPCA had no previous history of her. She had come to them from an animal sanctuary in Southport without any documents.

Last Sunday, when she bit so hard, I had determined that I could not keep her. But I feel sorry for her; she has settled

5

in so well, regards this as her home and the prospect of her having to start again in the cat's home would be awful for her and make me very sad.

I am extremely fond of her, so she is having a second chance.

Perhaps some steel gloves are needed.

And no, it isn't when I am playing with her. She is a softy then. She retrieves white mouse and drops him at my feet so that I can send him hurtling across the floor or up the stairs again.

But she is a hunter and I think unexpected movement has a lot to do with it.

Here is a picture of a very relaxed girl; can't you just see all that white hair coming out?

I'll send updates when time allows,

Love Jeanie xxx

Why Not?

You don't have a future. Why are you adopting a cat?

Companionship, a need to look after, a kindly act.

You were thinking of going into a care home yourself.

Would they have allocated you one, if they knew?

No eyes, no teeth, no feet. Blood cells turning bad.

How long do you think before you can't see her?

She is only two, she could live another ten years; more.

Angela is my age; she's just taken on a pair of kittens.

When they're fifteen she'll be ninety. You're both barmy.

A queen, you'll spend the rest of your life a handmaiden.

She'll never make a cup of tea. Wash up or cook dinner.

Demanding attention she'll wake you, well before ten.

And expensive: litter, food, vets, and sometimes a cattery.

I've changed my mind; I'll have two dogs instead.

Puss in a Box

Puss strikes a chord with someone, a family squabbling.

Blood letting. Boil lancing. It was a poem meant to strike

a balance, weighing against possible yellow tweeness.

It contained a few scattered unpleasant references

to human issues. It had no potential, no recommendations.

But now puss is going to materialise. Take form, shape.

Ophelia is coming to join me. I hope she knows her place.

There is only room for one Queen in this house.

She looks lovely, sounds great, isn't needy, unstressed.

The thing she asks, well, demands, is to be the only cat.

Like me, a friendly, loving, lady who wants all the fuss.

An arrival date is unknown but she'll be delivered in a box.

I can't wait to see puss coming out. Stepping cautiously,

beautiful, curious, alert. And yellow? No black and white.

Deserved

Thinking I'd like a cat, could offer a good loving home,

a large house, big garden, plenty of space, room,

there must be one out there in need, I searched.

Several websites had a selection of felines, appealing.

I was offered one called Sooty Sue, ten year old female,

black, sweet-natured, timid; two previous owners,

both elderly men who had died. Poor girl.

It was felt by the re-homers that she was my perfect match.

I wasn't sure being neither sweet nor timid by nature myself.

I turned her down. Just from a photo I chose you.

An over-confident, loud-mouthed, prey-hunting gobbler.

An unthinking pouncer. I am reminded of the saying;

If it's right for you it will come to you.

Have I got what I deserve?

The Annoyance of Beasts

She's full of character, a delight

but she has some annoying qualities:

not only does she bite,

she also vomits on the carpet.

It isn't endearing.

A supply of disposable gloves is needed.

Jay-cloths, disinfectant, stain-remover.

I am probably the only woman on the Wirral

who can live with her.

He/She whichever is appropriate

is possibly worse, certainly similar.

Loves to hide, pull strings, play tricks.

Run me round in circles.

Drive me barmy.

Rolling in frustration on the carpet.

Taking swipes and bites whenever they want.

No use, to me, bleach or caustic soda.

I could swear the two of them are in collusion.

Ophelia Untangled

From the moment

she stepped out

of the travelling basket

it was Her house

she owned it

self-assured

confident,

Quickly becoming acquainted with each chair

the feeding quarters and toy box, my lap.

Tin tack sharp

dauntless

she crouches intrigued

in front of the vacuum cleaner

ready to spring.

Unafraid of anything.

Loving a fuss.

She bit me.

Drew blood.

An attempt to jump up onto the laptop

where I was typing

I had stopped.

Ophelia had been thwarted.

She rubbed round my legs

rolled at my feet

appealingly.

I put down my hand to stroke her.

She sank her teeth into my hand

making it bleed in two places,

above and below,

bottom and top tooth marks.

Had it been a hunting ploy,

rolling on her back, open armed

waiting for the prey to come to her.

Or merely a bad habit

a failure to learn civil behaviour

the reason she was up for adoption.

I tell her constantly she's a good girl,

I've no doubt she believes me.

People make suggestions;

it was the unexpected,

she's deaf,

startled,

mistreated in the past,

primal fears,

feral living,

the hunter coming out,

over-excited, thought it was food, a defensive instinctive reaction.

I could psycho-analyze her all night.

No.

How about

bad temper,

spite,

domination,

revenge.

To show me who was boss.

Seeing me as a live-in carer.

Today she went for her booster vaccination.

Settled down, went to sleep in the carrier

on the way there and on the way back.

Unstressed.

She behaved impeccably,

the vaccinators described her as an angel.

I think we still both need to work on that.

The RSPCA website had said

she couldn't live with another cat.

Cat and Beast

Don't bite the hand that feeds you.

Good advice. For cat and beast.

If you do, move, or be moved, on.

Know when you're well off.

Satisfied with your lot. Strive to keep it.

Sinking your teeth into my flesh is not the way,

no matter how wonderful your other qualities;

how appealing, how endearing, how much fun.

They don't, can't, won't erase the teeth marks.

A disguise, granny's nightdress, a black and white coat,

a pretended air of love and goodwill

but the teeth like sharp daggers

always ready to unexpectedly sink.

Permanent, my beautiful Ophelia, fantastic beast,

is only a word. It doesn't necessarily apply to you.

Morning Ophelia

I tell her I know she's there.

She sleeps in the kitchen conservatory.

Behind a closed door.

If it wasn't, there'd be no chance of her staying there.

Plenty of room, biscuits, water, toys, easy chairs.

As I come downstairs in the morning

she hears me; piteously cries,

I'm in here; someone's mistakenly locked the door.

As it opens, the meow changes to warm greeting,

she tells me about her night.

We go to the sitting room, cuddle and purr.

Watch the news headlines.

I suggest she go back in the kitchen, put on the kettle.

She never does but I always ask.

She is happy and contented until I go in the kitchen.

Then seeing the empty food bowl she realises she's starved.

Contrariness

With your paws, you move balls around a plastic container

from which you can never hope to remove them.

Fascinated. A soft bodied, long-tailed, white mouse

you drop at my feet hoping I'll make her run across

the room. You watch expectantly, ready to dart after.

Catch. Return triumphant. Sometimes if you're lucky

she dashes across the hall floor, flies up the stairs.

Or into the conservatory where she lands in a box

with a hole in the top and cat-sized access doorways.

That is on the days I'm a good shot. She is never lost.

Except when you deliberately push her under the sofa.

You ignore the scratching dome especially bought,

at cost, for your use, preferring to shred the carpet.

Get under my feet if I'm busy, always anxious to help.

Sit on my lap if I'm writing, chest if I'm on the phone;

face upturned as close as you can get it to mine.

I spit cat hair. Otherwise, on the best seat you can find.

Cry loudly for food if the bowl is empty, refuse to eat

when it is filled. Scratch frantically at doors that are closed, when opened decline to go through. Scrupulously clean

you have no hesitation about vomiting on the carpet.

Want isolation on the litter tray, allow me no privacy

in mine. Delighted in the morning to see me after a night

alone but if I leave you for two hours while out shopping,

buying cat food, you refuse to speak when I get home.

Leaping

You crouch low on the paving stones

one side of the pond. On the opposite side

stands a thirsty pigeon. The enemy.

Through closed glass doors in the sitting room

I watch. Try to warn you. You won't do it.

Travelling seven feet, even for you, impossible.

You leap, it's a magnificent leap,

you clear the pond wall, rock surround,

travel three feet, plunge into the water.

Submerge. Turn tail, rapidly jump out.

Pond water scattering the patio. Embarrassed.

Have to be towel dried in the conservatory.

A lesson learnt?

I suspect no. I suspect not.

My headstrong, impulsive Ophelia.

Damned If She Will

She's damned if she'll use the scratching post

that has been bought specially for her.

Not while the carpet's so handy.

I show her how to do it. Ruin my nails.

Drawing my fingernails down the coiled rope.

She watches. I knew when I bought it

there was only a slim chance that she would.

Put outside it could be a boot-scraper.

Dome shaped with a covered bell on the top,

it would be quite amusing.

When it's outside used by we humans,

I have no doubt she'll be interested. Clawing.

Scraping off the mud; bringing it in the house.

Trails on conservatory floor, trodden into carpet.

Unwelcome

There are two cats who come into the garden.

Up until today she and they hadn't met.

They come separately. A grey and white tabby,

who I named Prince Louis, not after William

and Kate's son; rather because next door to

my daughter lives Princess Leia; so

Prince Louis came into my mind as fitting for him.

The other predominantly black, a few white markings.

Unnamed. I didn't mind them prowling.

It wasn't often; neither of them strays.

It was inevitable that one day she'd meet them.

Instantly hate. No chance of making friends.

I was in the kitchen, heard the fight.

They were on the conservatory doorstep,

he on his back she standing over him

having let go when I appeared. He took his chance

to bolt, she tore after him. I sat on the bench,

waited her reappearance. Nervous. Apprehensive.

Would there be blood. Dripping from her flank: Hers.

Dripping from her mouth: His. Neither.

She was triumphant because he had gone.

I congratulated her. We await the Prince.

Just Awful

I feel just awful.

I've booked her into a cattery.

Three times in a five week period.

She'll hate it. Sulk.

"Has she been in a cattery before?"

She hasn't.

But has come from the RSPCA,

so is used to confinement.

Will she think she's gone back there?

Waiting to be re-homed?

Will she trust me?

I'll send her with her white mouse

and crinkly multi-coloured unicorn.

They might comfort.

No mouse or unicorn will console me.

I'll feel just awful all holiday.

What if she isn't unhappy?

What if she likes it better there?

What if she doesn't want to come home?

Then I'll feel much worse.

Hunger

You meow for food

even when there is still some in your bowl.

A pitiful sound, thinking I can't see it.

When you decide nothing else is coming,

you eat it. I hear a crunching sound.

I knew I wasn't wrong.

Of course, if you were more cunning

you'd store it in cheek pouches like a hamster;

then you might get more.

The woman at the cattery assures me

that as well as your two main meals a day,

biscuits will be available at all times.

With you I suggest that there isn't an endless supply

or, you'll come back more of a barrel than you already are.

I may send you with pre-measured food.

Say you have special dietary requirements:

allowed to eat no more than your body weight

in any twenty-four hours.

Sticks

My curiosity is piqued. I am going to investigate.

Your conviction that something is under there

is so strong. I hope you weren't having me on.

The cupboard area extends six feet, then

turns a corner, another cupboard meets up

with the cooker. Impossible to access all areas.

Although I think you may have done, tunneling

beneath like a miner at the coal face or a caver,

edging intrepidly through the smallest rock space.

Uncle Bertie had a thin walking cane with a crook

handle. I'm down on my hands and knees with that.

I'm hoping for a family of shriveled mice.

Long dead. Mummified. Explaining your obsession.

Like an archaeologist, discovering, excavating a tomb.

The stick was used in the past to retrieve Pamela

hamster when she had escaped from her cage.

Over one night she had removed all her bedding,

set up camp behind a large chest of drawers;

a well constructed nest lodged halfway between

drawers and wall. We were going on holiday that day.

Luckily we recovered her with the help of Bertie's stick.

Nothing this time appears.

Friends

"What's a pussy cat saying then?

What is she telling me?"

I encourage her with questions.

I'm interested, want to hear more;

we both have a need to talk.

Recount, confide, and explain

Her vocabulary is limited.

I understand.

She's telling me she loves me.

She's telling me she's my friend.

It's only annoying when I'm paying

close attention to something else.

She can't know, doesn't understand.

She hasn't got an off button

I can't mute her.

I wouldn't if I could.

Re-reading this, written during the lockdown, I take back
every word – I'd mute her if I could!

Fearless

The shed roof is not easily accessed

being a long way off the ground.

Ophelia manages it.

Sits at each corner in turn; paces over the apex roof.

proud of this first time achievement.

Regal. I fear she will be stuck there.

Will I have to use the ladder

or call the fire brigade?

I didn't see how she got there.

I can't see how she'll get down.

Cutting back a bush in the garden;

she had been interestedly watching.

Then found something more exciting.

Scaling the shed. Viewing me from above.

She swells with pride; can you do this?

Getting down? She does it easily.

Butterfly

No, Ophelia don't tell me it was her own fault.

She didn't provoke you. She wasn't asking for it.

It was your fault entirely. Are you not ashamed?

Ophelia, you are a killer. Did you not think it would die?

Don't tell me you were playing.

They don't like being batted. Caught in your mouth.

Ophelia they're delicate. A word you don't understand.

Yes, it was stupid.

Came far too close. Tempting a black and white cat.

But, believe it or not, Ophelia they have

even smaller brains than you.

And yes, you are instinctive. Acted without thinking.

Had never seen one before. Wondered what it would do.

Had enough sense not to show me.

Won't ever do it again?

Bad Ophelia

You were outside. Alone. A lovely day.

My friend at the window watching and talking to me.

My friend shouted, 'No!' Too late.

You either take no notice or don't hear.

'She's caught a butterfly.'

The unfortunate creature had made the mistake

of fluttering too close to the ground in your vicinity.

Enjoying the early spring sunshine. You didn't hesitate.

'She's bringing her in to show you.'

But when you reached me you were empty mouthed.

Excitedly anxious to tell me.

I listened. Then said, 'Bad Ophelia.'

I found her a little while later.

Put in a corner. Placed where you could easily see her.

A trophy. Like a big cup in a glass wall-cabinet.

My friend picked her up, dropped her in the bin.

She had been a big brightly coloured one.

Cat Woman

I've turned into a cat lady.

At a moggie's beck and call.

Clothes all covered in cat hair.

Carpets all clawed and torn.

Speaking a different language – silly cat talk.

Plastic gloves and wet wipes – down on all fours

cleaning the mud stains left by dirty paws.

Removing solids from the litter tray.

If the other lady's chosen to sleep on my lap

taking very good care not to move. Disturb.

Throwing toy mice to amuse, jingling bells,

waving sticks with furry tails. Rolling balls.

Opening a door when she needs it

and even, because she's contrary, when she does not.

Grooming. Stroking. Do I smell of cat?

Buzz Off

My reckless Ophelia, I dread the sound of one coming in:

The buzzers, mad-fliers who drive you barmy, barmy as
them.

Giving chase in a heedless, reckless, pursuit. Determined

to catch them. You after them, me after you. Alarmed

you'll be stung or worse, break one of the ornaments which

stand unseen, unnoticed in your path. Delicate footed,

careful as you usually are, when angry, red-mist in your eyes

they become impeding useless objects; to me home-
enhancing

precious treasures. I watch in horror as they're flung aside.

Try to stop you. Impossible. Decide it's best to join in.

Hope it's a bluebottle fly, not a wasp making the noise.

You love it; the lioness in you enjoys a joint kill. Bonding.

It reinforces your belief you're doing the right thing.

Relief when they decide to fly away: sanctuary outdoors.

Wild Cat

Delicious warm days. Open windows. Open doors.

The garden's awakened but so have the flies.

Buzzing bluebottles, wasps, bees. Fine in the garden.

I dread them flying indoors. Bees stay in the conservatory

are easily caught 'neath a plastic jug, released outdoors.

Flies penetrate the interior, curious as to what they will find.

Ophelia, ever alert, fiercely possessive, doesn't tolerate

an intruder, no matter how small, especially one making a noise.

Raising her hackles still further the stupid things goad;

'Catch me if you can.' And she is determined the interloper

to see gone. A bounty hunter. Wanted. Dead or Alive.

They actually don't have that option: with Ophelia it's dead.

Disregarding the instruction not to knock anything over.

House rules. Concentrating only on the catch. Darting.

Springing onto surfaces, over furniture, leaping-up windows.

Overwhelmed by the need to catch the fiend. Destroy.

Luckily even the most stupid fly has so far disappeared.

Perhaps dropped behind the TV. A heart attack. Died from fear.

Wild Fifi

Mostly poetry is about the heart, usually anguished,

noble animals, often endangered, sweet, healing nature,

threatened with destruction. None of which I find possible.

That is until I acquired a cat, the beautiful Ophelia.

Wild Fifi. Capturing her nature, my heart, my frequent
anguish.

I have become or try to be a lion tamer. Domesticator.

When I first had her she was a biter. A nasty habit. Testing

who was dominant. I have talked her out of it.

We've cleared the air. Settled the matter. She's second.

I'm first. She is my right-hand woman. It makes her happy.

Assumes control when I'm absent. Head of the guard.

Protects me. A role she relishes. Patrolling house and garden.

Squaring up to all-comers. Accepting being second doesn't

make her inferior. Love. Respect. The feeling is mutual.

Unpredictable Mowers

Sometimes I am the one who protects her.

She is terrified of the lawn mower.

I keep it at bay.

She flees in the house.

I forbid it to follow.

Assure her I won't let it hurt her.

She peeps out. Unsure.

Grows a bit bolder.

Watches from a safe place.

Ready to bolt if approached.

I wrestle with the machine.

Too far forward I pull it back.

Stronger than it, though I can't stop its roar.

Cutting finished.

Cord winding.

She follows the plug as it runs across the lawn.

Like me, she does love the smell of the cut grass.

Wholesome Diets

A plain diet, not fancy food is what suits you best.

Meat or fish flakes in jelly, dry biscuits, water.

Convent food. Plain and wholesome.

A repast at regular hours is fallen on with gratitude.

Apportioned in a bowl. Not self-served.

A rich diet causes you problems, vomiting

and worse. Give thanks for what you're given.

Some poor cats have nothing at all.

They'd be glad for half of what you're given.

The fat cats, rich diets, gravy, custard, cream,

will regret their overindulgence, blocked arteries,

gout, bad dreams. Obese, unfit, unattractive.

That isn't the diet of an athlete. Superwoman.

Better to be as you are: a sensibly well-fed girl.

Sooty Sue

I feel guilty about poor Sooty Sue.

I hope she was adopted, given a third chance.

Turned down by me, in favour of you.

She was ten years, you only twelve months.

People want kittens, six weeks to six months.

Playful. Cute. Able to learn good habits.

Not yet having acquired any bad.

The danger of adopting a stray. Or, unwanted.

Thrown out for being an incorrigible scally.

Sooty Sue was none of these. Blameless.

She simply had the misfortune that two of her

owners died. She was steady and serious.

Unsure why she was there. Where were the men

who had loved her? Where now could she turn?

Would she have been better suited to me?

Who then would have been better suited to you?

Little Cat

We think of each other as big cat and little cat.

I prefer that to young and old.

She is sometimes deferential, when she remembers.

There does seem to be an unwritten rule,

she leaves me alone when I'm eating,

my food bowl is clearly off limits, as is hers.

She never sits in my chair unless I am in it

then she unhesitatingly sits on my lap.

She always has to prove she is faster downstairs.

Has keener sight, smell and reflexes.

Wonders how I am in charge. What makes her second.

Well Fifi perhaps it's because you can't open doors;

or access your own food. She watches in amazement

as I open the food packet, sealed in a sachet

she can neither see it nor smell it. Magic.

I move my hands and there it is.

My rightful place is maintained.

Cabbage White

I saw you sitting on your back legs reaching

with your front paws, trying to catch that Cabbage White.

An innocent visitor, hovering near the low blossom

which he genuinely didn't know was yours.

You streaked the length of the garden after him;

running as fast as he could fly. Delighted.

Then lost him as he gained height; went next door.

Fifi, he may come back, or one just like him.

Think hard about this: you are not to hurt him.

No, not even if you get the chance.

It isn't you or him. A feud. A duel.

The victor is not the Cat's Whiskers.

Remember Cabbage Whites are our friends.

Back Then

In Egypt's early days, you'd have been venerated,

slept on an embroidered couch, fed from a golden bowl.

Fanned if you were too hot, warmed if you were cold.

Ophelia, nothing would have been too much trouble.

Mummified when you died. Placed in a splendid tomb.

Does your accumulative memory stretch back that far?

Because it's the Ancient Egyptians who I blame for

creating the modern moggie who we serve today.

They gave you and your kind, Fifi, very big ideas

that we have to try and live up to. Strive. Do our best.

We don't always succeed in meeting your demands.

A sunny garden, luxurious home, food on demand.

Unlimited respect and attention from your very own slave.

Total devotion. Supporting your ideas on self-worth.

The Egyptians had a cat god with a gold earring, Bast.

But my poor Fifi I'm afraid you'll find times have changed.

Birthday

You don't have a known birthday

Unless someone sends you a card we may never know it.

We must settle for Jan 26th the day you arrived here.

It isn't very convenient being so soon after Christmas.

Never mind. Age is more difficult.

The RSPCA made a guess at two. A stab in the dark.

The vet thought much younger

And so do I. Not much more than one I should say.

The vet checked you for any possible physical problems,

health issues, ailments, malfunctions, things of that kind.

His opinion was you were a superb specimen, though

overweight. A little heavy. Something that hasn't changed.

Someone referred to you as a pinhead.

'You're a plumpy dumpy,' I constantly tell you, which is

something I would not say to many, being far too polite.

Do you really want to be the fattest cat in the
neighbourhood?

You waddle. Eat less, exercise more, or at least hold it in.

Move

Do you like it when I have to step round you?

Do you feel empowered?

Do you sit there on purpose?

Do you think I have no choice?

She runs in front, sits, waits.

'Move' I cajole. 'Keep going.'

She appears not to hear.

'Let me through, I'll give you some biscuits.'

Resorting to bribery once again.

I step awkwardly to one side. Squeeze through the door.

She follows. Overtakes. Waits expectantly in the kitchen

next to her empty bowl. 'You promised.'

'No, I tried to strike a bargain. You refused.'

Her face falls. I open the cupboard door.

Well-being

When a professional gives it as his opinion

that you're overweight; need to lose some

then you really should take heed.

Listen. Act before it's too late to pull back.

Problems could lie ahead, do you

want to become too heavy for your legs?

Buckle. Have breathing difficulties. Wheezing.

Heart problems. Palpitations. Flatulence.

Constipation. Haemorrhoids. Bad breath.

Needing help to get upstairs or out of bed.

Unable to get over the fence. Up the tree.

Do you want the pigeons to laugh at you?

Call names. Sneer. Jeer. Show their contempt.

Stay where they are on the lawn. Pull faces.

Bathe in the pond which you are supposed to guard.

It's alright being cocky while you're young and healthy.

Shall we start today by cutting out elevenses?

Before

Ophelia, where were you before?

Why did you need to be re-housed?

Is there someone searching for their princess?

Is there a family glad to see you gone?

Someone cared enough to have you spayed.

Were they no longer able to care for you?

Why weren't you micro-chipped?

When you're restless are you thinking of a previous home?

Were you abandoned, lived for a time outdoors?

A home-body, well trained, that's not how you were raised.

You are not an alley cat. What were you called?

Were there other cats? Did you fight?

Was someone allergic? Did they emigrate?

Were you a soon tired-of Christmas present?

Ophelia, did you bite?

Quiet, Ophelia?

Quiet days are something I've given up on

since acquiring a cat.

Silence with Ophelia just isn't possible.

She's the noisiest cat I've known.

They told me she was noisy, well, in so many words,

'She's talked to me all the way,

you've got a character there.'

Since then she hasn't stopped talking,

telling me what she's seen, thought, smelt, done,

oh and what she's heard.

Tells me when she's going to use the litter tray

and when she has done.

Comments on what I am wearing.

Asks who's on the phone.

Why do I sit so long at the laptop?

When she wants to play.

Tells me to turn the tv off, music or talking books.

I'm relieved and so pleased when she says

it's time to go to bed.

Hunger Pangs

She goes in the garden for five minutes

then is back to tell me what she has done.

Looked in the pond, jumped onto the fence, run on the grass.

That she's heard birds. The state of the weather.

If I am using the laptop that drives her barmy.

Am I listening? Does she have my attention?

She thinks not. Becomes louder, more insistent. Worse.

Changes the subject. Asks for food. Pitiful.

She's deprived and hungry. Famished. Starved.

She can hold out no longer; she's going to expire.

Desperate begging. Plaintive mewing. It's lies.

She's not long been fed. But I'm exasperated.

I head for the kitchen. She runs ahead. And waits.

Naughty minx. There's food still in the bowl. She eats.

Twitcher

Your claims to be a bird lover I don't believe;

although I know you do find them attractive.

Watch alertly. Crouch. Stalk. Give chase.

They seem not to be attracted to you.

Flying fast as soon as they realise you are

on the prowl. Hunter's pose. Bad intent.

Body tense. Face set. Green eyes fixed.

Alarm. Flight. Putting air between them and you.

And if you caught one what would you do?

Make friends? Play? A conversation.

Then let him go? Ophelia, I don't think so.

A bird watcher. A twitcher. A fancier. Yes.

Fascinated. Absorbed. Obsessed.

But your claims to be a bird lover; Ophelia, no.

Identity

Even with my dark glasses on you know me.

My smell, touch, sound, are the same.

The dark glasses don't fool you.

I wonder if there's anything I could do.

Would a false beard confuse you?

You'd still recognise my smell, touch, sound.

A mouse smelling beard, covering my mouth,

producing a muffled. squeaking sound.

Touch? Well, obviously hairy hands needed too.

In a chase I would come off worse;

unable to squeeze under the door, behind

the cupboard, fridge or cooker.

In fact no appliances at all. Outwitted. Discovered.

A fraud. A woman in mouse clothing.

Would you laugh? Would our positions reverse?

Me no longer in the dominant position.

Do I really want to be taken for a mouse?

Poppy

One of the great pleasures in life is owning a cat.

So other cat owners tell me.

I'm sure they mean it. I have Ophelia.

She does her best. I try harder.

The poor girl's problem is I've known Poppy.

She's unfairly compared. Poppy being the most

wonderful pussy-cat. He lived here with me

for four months while his owners moved house.

Before that I had known him for twelve years.

Most lovable, friendliest, sweetest, best.

A lot to live up to. Poor Ophelia struggles.

She'd hate him. The jealous, possessive creature.

He and I now have to meet in secret.

Like Peter Pan he's never grown up, still a kitten nature.

Compared to him Ophelia is a stroppy teenager.

Flaunting her independence, still playing with toys.

Curiously exploring, confident, know it all.

Sometimes in need of rescuing. Reassuring cuddles.

Of course, really I adore her, and at least I don't

have to keep her in mobile phone minutes or clothes.

Not Homage

This isn't a homage to Ophelia.

Her bad qualities balance her good.

I love her but that doesn't cloud my judgement.

Faults and best qualities both must be acknowledged.

A balanced picture presented of her character.

Our relationship as seen by her and me.

The ups and downs of life together.

Smooth. Turbulent. Good. Bad.

What would we do if not together?

This is something which only I think about.

Ophelia confidently accepting the situation.

That this is how it will always be.

Her and I; neither of us changing

or needing to. Acceptance. A partnership.

Destiny. What else? I know she's right.

Do I regret it? Blessing or curse?

Divination

When I go to pass water, as Aunt Eth used to say,

use the loo, she wants to come with me. Cheeky cat.

No doubt thinking if she could sniff my urine

more closely she'd understand me better.

Decide if she likes me or not. Am I male or female.

What sort of character I've got. Temperament gleaning.

Why I don't use a litter tray like any decent cat.

Poor training. A lackadaisical upbringing.

Taken from my mother too soon. Lack of maternal advice.

Or simply stubborn resistance. Now possibly too late.

A keen sense of smell is indispensible for divining.

Will it tell her why I can eat when I like

while she cannot? Decide when she goes to bed.

Knowledge is power. I keep the door closed.

Harmony

Don't think for one moment

that I'm claiming she's a wonderful cat.

In tune with my every thought; movement.

She's not a dog. Woman's best friend.

Whenever I leave my chair she doesn't think walkies

but that I must be going to feed her.

Disappointment as so often for dogs follows.

Harmony? Yes, sometimes, exceptional moments.

But we are companions, sharing a home.

Our lives. For better or worse. In sickness and health.

Not taking each other for granted.

Respectful. Interested. Connecting.

Not taking advantage. Not playing tricks.

Well, at least on my side we are.

Bad Days

How long will the animal be left alone?

That is one of the questions the RSPCA ask.

As long as possible is the answer.

She may hope to see me sometime next year.

This isn't true. The longest I've left her is

two hours; she doesn't speak to me when I return.

Has her own idea about what time is decent,

how long a cat can reasonably be expected to wait.

Pretends she doesn't know me. Never seen me before.

She sits and washes. Nonchalance in every lick.

Only when I approach the food-bowl does she stir.

Show an interest. Tell me she's missed me.

Loves me. Couldn't wait for me to get back.

I replenish the biscuits. Eagerly, she turns her back.

Carcasses

I walk past the dead bird on the floor.

Assume it's one of the cat's toys.

Brown mouse comes to mind.

Four mice and a unicorn,

are randomly scattered around the house.

My foot moves it out of the way.

It has been dropped in the dining room doorway.

White mouse is in the hall, under the radiator.

Smart mouse in the kitchen; blue unicorn the conservatory.

None causing a problem. Until,

a visitor sees the dead bird. Horror.

Feet in the air surrounded by loose feathers.

Disposable gloves, a dustpan and brush,

a calming cup of tea and biscuit.

How lucky I hadn't bent to pick it up.

Carrion

Fifi! How could you bring it in the house?

No! Don't tell me in your mouth.

That is disgusting. A young bird.

Hardly any life behind, now none before.

A few months old, perhaps a summer hatchling.

Brought in the house, dropped on the dining room floor.

I thought it was one of your toys – brown mouse.

Someone else spotted it – your disgrace,

my humiliation, their horror.

Fluffy feathers scattered, small feet in the air.

A sweet looking little corpse.

We photographed him to preserve his memory.

A dustpan and brush removed him to the bin.

Ophelia, you watched curiously – unabashed.

Cutie

'Granny, your cat is such a cutie.'

Later, Fifi, you bit her because she sat on your sofa.

We watched as you rolled in the long grass,

pounced on things that weren't there,

entertainingly chased your tail. Climbed the apple tree

beneath which we both were working.

Cleverly balanced, walked along the branches.

Maggie's not sure you can get down.

Thinks you need help, unsure how to do it.

'Shall I help her?' 'No if she got up she can get down.'

When I return, Fifi, you are on the ground.

'I did have to help her she was swinging by her front claws.'

Fifi, you actress, you drama queen.

Your agility is legendary, you go up that tree every day.

How kind of someone to help you down.

'Granny your cat is such a cutie.'

Later you bit her arm, she's not so sure now.

Bonfire Night

Sleeping comfortably with a full tummy,

The date on the calendar is lost on you.

Outside a firework goes off with a bang.

You raise your head from the sofa.

Annoyed. Look around for someone to bite.

Show your disapproval, express your displeasure.

There is only me; you think better of it.

Settle back, ignore further bangs.

Your self-assurance is what I expected.

Anxiety not in your self-confident nature.

Getting off the sofa, seeking the hands

of those lighting the blue touch papers

to nip the flesh and so teach them a lesson?

Well, it really just wasn't worth the effort.

Built In

Fifi, there has been a programme on the television

concerning interesting finds in old buildings: house and
church;

hidden beneath floors, between walls, roof spaces, chimneys,

what are thought to be protective charms.

Amongst other things bent iron nails, written curses,

fat-bellied, narrow-necked bottles which once contained

urine, hair hanks, finger nail clippings, and cats.

Preserved bodies of your feline brothers and sisters;

placed there apparently to keep evil, especially witchcraft,
out.

Ironic, since most self-respecting witches kept a cat.

Would you once have flown on a broomstick?

Or been interred in a brick tomb?

Safe-guarding the premise: keeping want and trouble out.

Some when found still have coloured hair.

Scratch marks show that when placed not all were dead.

Poor creatures. Cruel thatchers, carpenters, masons.

Fifi, thank your lucky stars you live in kinder, less
superstitious times.

Diabolical

Ophelia, old women have been known to swallow cats,

that is after they have swallowed spiders.

It isn't inevitable or a common occurrence.

An old wives' tale, an oral tradition, a remedy

for the wriggling and tickling inside them.

But worse, Ophelia, they then swallow a dog.

A dog is something you have never yet encountered.

Ungainly brutes who cannot balance on fences.

The dull oafs of the animal kingdom.

Jealous, feeble-minded, deniers of cats' superiority.

They exist merely to plague you.

If you see one, run and seek safety in a tree.

Tree climbing is a skill they haven't yet mastered,

concentrating on sit, wait, walk to heel, play dead:

people pleasing tricks you wouldn't dream of doing.

The idea of swallowing one to chase a cat is diabolical.

Catty

No, Ophelia, I am not easily driven barmy.

When I say you are driving me it, take heed.

Don't call me a grumpy old woman

when I say a cat does not need to eat every five minutes.

I am not a monster when I refuse to refill the food bowl.

And no-one likes to be called a miserable old hag.

Yes, I do do what, in my opinion, is in your best interests.

We disagree on how much and how often you should eat.

It doesn't make me a hard-hearted fiend.

Calling me names will do you no good.

Ophelia, there's a name for women like you – catty.

Inspiring

Fifi, you inspire me to write poetry.

It's therapy; a way of coping.

Cheaper than a psychiatrist,

a long term stay in a clinic or a luxury holiday.

A means of baring my soul, getting it off my chest.

A steam release valve.

A spirit level, keeping my bubble in the middle.

Written words detail our relationship.

The joy, the pain, the struggle to accept,

The fun, the frustration, of living with a naughty cat.

Would you like the chance to answer back?

Name Changing

Fifi is pronounced Feefee

and not Fie fie

It doesn't rhyme with pie

it rhymes with me

the perfect name for you

I should have called you Meme.

I very well may.

Different Fish

In the last ten years the only pets I've kept have been fish.

They've suited me. Quiet, unobtrusive, self-contained.

Rather than two years of life, as predicted by the petshop

they lived for eight. I should have replaced them.

I had the tank. Instead wanting something warm-blooded

I got a cat. Ophelia. The fish were silent; she is not.

The fish were happy being fed once a day.

They looked forward to it. Ophelia has an insatiable appetite.

Piteously asks, turns shirty when denied.

The fish were calming. Fifi entertaining. Curious. Playful.

The fish stayed in their tank. Fifi an explorer.

The fish undemanding. Fifi always seeking attention.

Annoying, loving, clawing the carpet seem to be

the main differences between fish and cats.

But mostly it's, 'my terms and no-one else's.'

Cats' Heaven

Pope Francis may have said animals go to Heaven

but, Fifi, we can't be sure he was talking about you;

he wasn't actually handing you a free pass in.

It still all depends on good behaviour while you're here.

God is probably watching you closely, writing things down.

The Lord loves the birds and butterflies, yes, Fifi,

they will be there in Heaven, along with dogs.

No Fifi, that won't make it Hell. God must be appalled

watching your wanton behaviour, heartless ways;

killing the weak and vulnerable, the small creatures,

the delicately formed who are there to be cherished;

as well as biting me and being sick on the dining room floor.

It all mounts up over time and counts against you in the end.

Yes, Fifi, God does care, He counts the sparrows on the
ground.

Hunting skills and a surly attitude won't be valued.

Fifi, like you God will have His own strong ideas.

Cat-Napping

Richard's cat, Hazel, sleeps peacefully on his bed.

Only a fool, Fifi, would share one with you.

Hazel, Richard's cat, wakes him every morning at eight

by gently licking his face and hands.

Your demands throughout the night would be constant.

To be fed, let out, given a cuddle.

Scratching at the door, jumping on the bedside table.

Demanding the light was on; demanding the light was off.

A peaceful night unobtainable.

Could you share a bed? Of course not.

As you rolled, stretched, invaded my decreasing space.

Pushed, shoved, I would end up on the floor.

Woken with a kiss? Woken with a bite?

Sleeping with the devil would be less trouble.

Courtship

Your only chance of matrimony, Fifi

- it is a very slim one –

Is if you meet an elegant owl

who hopefully will twit twoo you,

take you out sailing, show you his money,

play his guitar, sing songs of flattery.

Owls are well-known for liking cats.

They share a love of night time adventures.

Noisy calling throughout the neighbourhood.

Sharp eyes, sharp hearing, always looking for prey

And Fifi totally suited to you. Do you know why?

He can turn his head 180□when he doesn't want to see you.

Ancestry

Yes, Ophelia, I do know you're descended from sabre tooth tigers.

And I agree I am descended from apes.

But let's ask ourselves this - who invented fire?

And who is it now who pays the central heating bills?

You still have the best hunting skills, teeth, claws.

The patience to crouch for hours, pounce, catch in your jaws.

But how many chicken chunks in jelly packets

have you opened; poured into your bowl?

I haven't noticed many cats pushing trolleys in Tesco

or struggling to carry boxes of Sheba home.

You have more in your food cupboard than I have in mine.

So let's try, Ophelia to show some gratitude.

If it wasn't for us, you'd still be living in the wild.

Your brains got smaller and smaller; ours have grown and grown.

Apes are no longer numbskulls in the animal world

and sabre tooth tigers have learned how to purr.

John Philip

There's a new cat on the block.

We've called him John Philip.

He wants to be friends.

He sits and looks through the window.

It drives Ophelia barmy.

Her growling doesn't faze him.

But then he does seem a dollop.

He is large, black and white, ugly.

Docile in the extreme. More than approachable.

He greets me on my return; wants to come in.

Is he a stray? I think not, he looks well fed.

But where does he sleep? I worry.

Would Ophelia let him have a bed in the conservatory?

He does seem love-struck, gazes adoringly at her.

But she, the hard-hearted minx, disdains him.

And it's difficult to see what he can do to win her over.

Devilish Company

Some people think cats are the companions of the devil, Fifi.

I don't think that about you.

Not unless the devil has the patience of a saint,

and a sense of humour too.

Restless

Ophelia, you are as restless as a cat on a hot tin roof.

Ants in your pants, always on the move.

An itching powder shirt.

In, out, then out again.

Why can't you settle? Relax?

What are you searching for?

You pace the garden paths. Prowl around the pond.

Come in and loudly meow.

It's a complaint but I don't know what you want.

What do you want?

Do you think of another location, other people?

Memories of your previous life.

Was it better there than here?

Only when curled on my lap do you chill.

Characteristics

You're the cat's whiskers,

is a compliment, Fifi,

while you are the dog's testicles isn't.

Hawk eyes, pig's ears, donkey droppings.

Hyena's grin, hungry as a horse.

Sly as a snake, cunning as a fox.

Noisy as a rook, prickly as a hedgehog.

Crazy as a frog, daft as a bat.

Of which Ophelia you are a mixture.

But yes, sometimes you are the cat's whiskers.

Last Word

'She's going then.'

"No! Why do you say that?"

'You've been overheard telling her.'

"Really! Where would she go?"

'Someone has offered to have her.'

"This is her home. She's happy here."

'Sometimes you tell her you can't live with her.'

"Take no notice of anything I say. She doesn't."

'Her being cloth-eared is one of the things you can't stand.'

"Yes along with being whiny and greedy."

'As well as demanding and attention-seeking.'

"Only when I'm trying to do something."

'So why do you keep her? Why isn't she going?'

"We've bonded. I love her."

ACKNOWLEDGEMENTS

Thank you to all the people who bought my first book, *Fairly Tall Tales*, and said kind things about it.

Thank you to Roanne, who has put together and proofread this book, Cat Chat.

Thank you to all the people who have been to this house over the past few years and, like myself, have put up with this recalcitrant cat. Thank you for your kindness and indulgence of her.

ABOUT THE AUTHOR

In the wild and woolly uplands of the Wirral, where Sir Gawain trekked this way and that, first this way and then that way, and never complained; where the people of Southport sent their wild beasts to be tamed, there lived a poet with a recalcitrant cat, of which much is to be learned in this book.

In my first book, *Fairly Tall Tales: not suitable for small people*, she only got the mildest mention of my living with her. In this book will be seen my stoicism, fortitude and good nature in putting up with her.

We are still together.

Printed in Great Britain
by Amazon

54939101R00042